A Zebra's World

written and illustrated by Caroline Arnold

PICTURE WINDOW BOOKS
Minneapolis, Minnesota

Special thanks to our advisers for their expertise:

Zoological Society of San Diego
San Diego Zoo
San Diego, California

Susan Kesselring, M.A., Literacy Educator
Rosemount–Apple Valley–Eagan (Minnesota) School District

Editor: Christianne Jones
Designer: Nathan Gassman
Page Production: James Mackey
Creative Director: Keith Griffin
Editorial Director: Carol Jones
The illustrations in this book were created with cut paper.

Picture Window Books
5115 Excelsior Boulevard
Suite 232
Minneapolis, MN 55416
877-845-8392
www.picturewindowbooks.com

Printed in the United States of America.

Library of Congress Cataloging-in-Publication Data
Arnold, Caroline.
A zebra's world / written and illustrated by
Caroline Arnold.
p. cm. — (Caroline Arnold's animals)
Includes bibliographical references.
ISBN 1-4048-1324-1 (hard cover)
1. Zebras—Juvenile literature. I. Title.

QL737.U62A762 2006
599.6657—dc22
2005023139

There are three kinds of zebras.
The zebras in this book are plains zebras.

Where plains zebras live: Africa

Habitat: open plains and grassy woodlands

Food: grass and low growing plants

Height: 4 feet (1.2 meters)

Weight: up to 550 pounds (248 kilograms)

Animal class: mammals

Scientific name: *Equus burchelli*

A baby zebra is called a foal. Follow a zebra foal as she grows up in Africa and learn about a zebra's world.

The sun rises over the African plain. Zebras wake up and sniff the fresh morning air. There is a new member of the herd. She is just a few hours old.

Soon, the baby zebra and her mother will join the rest of the herd in their daily search for fresh, green grass.

A newborn zebra weighs between 60 and 70 pounds (27 and 32 kg) and is about 3 feet (90 centimeters) tall.

A newborn zebra is able to stand within 20 minutes of birth.

6

The baby zebra bends her knees and struggles to stand. She takes a few wobbly steps. Soon, she gets her balance.

Now the young zebra can see the other zebras in the herd. They are looking for something to eat.

The young zebra is hungry, too. She nuzzles under her mother's warm belly and drinks some milk.

giraffe

elephants

Zebras share the African plains with giraffes, elephants, and many other animals.

The mother zebra keeps her baby close. She will not let any other zebras come near until the baby is a few days old.

Some of the other females in the herd have babies,
too. Each mother knows her own baby by its smell
and the pattern of its stripes.

The leader of the herd is a full-grown male zebra.
He protects the herd. He makes
sure that no one wanders
too far. He chases away
other zebras that are
not in his herd.

Plains zebras usually live in family herds of five to 20 animals. Each herd has one adult male plus several females and their foals.

A full grown zebra can eat up to 20 pounds (9 kg) of food a day.

The young zebra is now three weeks old. She eats grass for the first time. She bites off the blades with sharp front teeth.

Once a day, the young zebra and her mother follow the herd to a water hole. The thirsty zebras lap up the cool water. While some drink, others keep an eye out for danger.

Nearby, something rustles in a patch of tall grass. It's a lion!

"Kwa, kwa, kwa," calls out one of the zebras. Danger is near! The zebras take off across the plain. The young zebra gallops fast to keep up. Her hooves pound the hard ground.

lion

Day and night, zebras must look out for lions, wild dogs, cheetahs, and other meat eaters. Zebras can outrun most predators.

As the herd flees, the zebras call to one another.
They make sure that no one gets left behind.

Exercise helps a young
zebra's muscles grow strong.

16

The young zebra is now four months old.
She plays with the other young zebras in
the herd.

The zebras push and shove one another.
They race across the plain. When they get
tired, they lay down to rest.

In most parts of Africa, the rainy season is during the spring and summer months. Near the equator, there are two short rainy seasons each year.

elephant

wildebeest

The young zebras were born in the rainy season. Now the rain has stopped. Water holes are drying up. It is time for the zebras to go to the river to find more water.

The zebras walk for many miles. Many family herds come together to form one giant herd. They see other thirsty animals at the river, too.

The zebras stay near the river until the rainy season comes again. Then the herds head back to the open plain to feast on new, green grass.

The young zebra is now a year old. She is able to take care of herself. Soon her mother will have a new baby. Then there will be another young zebra ready to run with the herd.

Where do zebras live?

Zebras live in Africa. The plains zebras live on open plains and in grassy woodlands throughout East Africa. They are the most common kind of zebra. Grevy's zebras live in dry semidesert areas of northern Kenya, Somalia, Ethiopia, and Sudan. Mountain zebras live in South Africa.

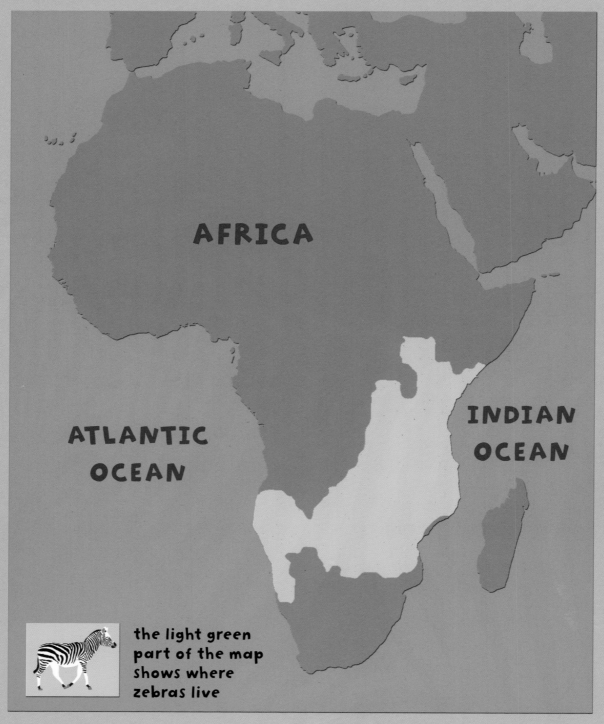

AFRICA

ATLANTIC
OCEAN

INDIAN
OCEAN

the light green
part of the map
shows where
zebras live

ZEBRA FUN FACTS

White with Stripes

Most scientists agree that zebras are white animals with black or brown stripes.

Original Stripes

Zebra stripes are like fingerprints. No two zebras are exactly alike. They can be used to tell one zebra from another.

Fast Runners

A zebra can gallop at speeds of more than 40 miles (64 km) per hour. Zebras can run long distances without tiring or slowing down.

Strong Teeth

A zebra has strong teeth for cutting and crushing grass. The molars, or chewing teeth, grow throughout a zebra's life.

Sharp Eyes

A zebra's eyes are set high on the head. Even when bending over to eat or drink, a zebra can see out over the plain and look for predators.

A Zebra's Life

Zebras can live to be more than 20 years old.

Glossary

blade—*a leaf of grass*

equator—*an imaginary line around the middle of Earth; it divides the northern half from the southern half*

gallop—*to run so fast that all four legs leave the ground at once*

habitat—*the place and natural conditions in which a plant or animal lives*

herd—*a family group of zebras*

lap—*to drink with the tongue*

mammals—*warm-blooded animals that feed their babies milk*

plain—*flat, grassy land with few trees*

predators—*animals that hunt and eat other animals*

To Learn More

At the Library

Penny, Malcolm. *Zebra: Habitats, Life Cycles, Food Chains, Threats.* Austin, Texas: Raintree Steck-Vaughn, 2003.

Schaefer, Lola M. Zebras: *Striped Grass-grazers.* Mankato, Minn.: Bridgestone Books, 2002.

Stewart, Melissa. *Zebras.* New York: Children's Press, 2002.

On the Web

FactHound offers a safe, fun way to find Internet sites related to this book. All of the sites on FactHound have been researched by our staff.

1. Visit *www.facthound.com*

2. Type in this special code for age-appropriate sites: 1404813241

3. Click on the FETCH IT button.

Your trusty FactHound will fetch the best sites for you!

Index

Look for all of the books in the Caroline Arnold's Animals series:

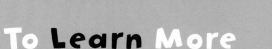